Washington Avenue Branch
Albany Public Library
NOV 0 7 2016

W9-DAI-615

A HOME IN THE BIOME

At Home in the
WETLANDS

Louise and Richard Spilsbury

PowerKiDS press
New York

Published in 2016 by **The Rosen Publishing Group**
29 East 21st Street, New York, NY 10010

Copyright © 2016 by The Rosen Publishing Group

All rights reserved. No part of this book may be reproduced in any form
without permission in writing from the publisher, except by a reviewer.

Produced for Rosen by Calcium
Editors: Sarah Eason and Amanda Learmonth
Designers: Paul Myerscough and Emma DeBanks

Picture credits: Cover: Shutterstock: Rob Hainer. Insides: Dreamstime: Ana Del
Castillo 4–5, Ckchiu 22–23, Kcmatt 19, Xidong Luo 28–29, _maximus_ 17, Steven
Prorak 14–15, Crystal Venters 7; Shutterstock: Greg Amptman 27, Bonnie Taylor
Barry 11, basel101658 10–11, George Burba 1, 13, Rich Carey 26–27, MF Choi
24–25, cvalle 5, 20–21, Karel Gallas 9, J. Helgason 6–7, Attila Jandi 23, jurra8
15, Heiko Kiera 21, leisuretime70 25, Chris Moody 8–9, optimarc 16–17, Vadim
Petrakov 12–13, Ray49 18–19, Sukpaiboonwat 29.

Cataloging-in-Publication Data
Spilsbury, Louise.
At home in the wetlands / by Louise and Richard Spilsbury.
p. cm. — (A home in the biome)
Includes index.
ISBN 978-1-5081-4569-1 (pbk.)
ISBN 978-1-5081-4570-7 (6-pack)
ISBN 978-1-5081-4571-4 (library binding)
1. Wetland ecology — Juvenile literature. 2. Wetlands — Juvenile literature.
3. Wetland animals — Juvenile literature. I. Spilsbury, Louise. II. Spilsbury, Richard,
1963-. III. Title.
QH541.5.M3 S75 2016
577.68—d23

Manufactured in the United States of America
CPSIA Compliance Information: Batch BW16PK: For Further Information contact Rosen Publishing, New York, New York at 1-800-237-9932

Contents

At Home in the Mud

A wetland is a place where the soil is soggy, because water reaches or covers the surface for most of the time. Wetlands can be covered by seawater or freshwater. Swamps, marshes, ponds, the edge of a lake or ocean, and the muddy land at the mouth of a river are all types of wetlands.

Difficult Places for Life

Wetland **biomes** are tricky places for wildlife to live. Some are wet for months or years, but then dry out completely. There is far less **oxygen** in mud than there is in soil, and plants rely on oxygen to get their food. Also, dead leaves **decay** very slowly in mud. This means that mud does not release the **nutrients** that help living things grow as well as they do in soil.

HOME SWEET HOME

Reeds are wetland plants that often grow with their lower parts under the water and their upper parts above it. They are tall, with narrow leaves that blow easily in the wind and bend in water so they are not damaged. Reeds have hollow stems that carry oxygen from the air to the plant parts underwater.

Tall reed plants have **roots** that spread wide and deep to anchor them in soft mud under the water.

Swamp
Cypresses

The plants that grow in wetlands need special adaptations to live in the wet conditions. Swamp forests are covered in trees, such as swamp cypresses, that are well-adapted to living in flooded soil.

Huge Tree Trunks

One feature of swamp cypresses stands out above all others. These trees look distinctive because the base of their tall trunks is swollen and huge. This helps the trees spread their roots over a wider area than would otherwise be possible. It is difficult to stay anchored in wet soils, so having a wide root base helps swamp cypresses stay upright and support the weight of their leaves and branches.

Bald cypress trees are named for their bald "knees," which do not have **bark**. This allows the trees to more easily absorb oxygen from the air.

HOME SWEET HOME

A cypress tree has special roots known as "knees." These grow upward from horizontal roots just below the water's surface, so that they stick out above it. There is little oxygen in the mud beneath the water, so the tree's knees grow above the water to take in oxygen from the air and carry it to the rest of the tree.

Venus FlytrapS

Most plants get the nutrients that help them grow from the soil they live in. As wetland soils are often low in nutrients, plants have to find other ways of surviving. There are a lot of insects in wetlands, so Venus flytrap plants catch and feed on these to survive.

Deadly Leaves

The leaves of the Venus flytrap can open and close like a mouth. At the end of the leaves are spikes, and inside the leaves are tiny hairs. When an insect lands on a leaf and touches the hairs, the leaf instantly closes. The spikes form a cage from which the insect cannot escape. The leaves close tighter to squash the **prey** and the plant makes a glue to seal the edge of the trap. Next, the Venus flytrap releases special substances that break down the insect's body so the plant can absorb it.

The Venus flytrap mainly catches and eats insects, but sometimes it traps small frogs too!

HOME SWEET HOME

The Venus flytrap's fast-moving, toothed leaves are green on the outside but red on the inside. Insects are attracted to the red color and when they land on the leaf, the Venus flytrap strikes.

Dragonflies

Dragonflies can survive only in wetlands. This is because they are born underwater and spend the first two years of their lives there.

Up and Away!

The **larvae** of dragonflies **hatch** from eggs and live and feed in water. They take in and squirt out jets of water to move themselves around. They eat **tadpoles**, fish, other insect larvae, and even each other! When it is time to leave the water, the larvae crawl up a plant stem and out of the water. Their outer skin breaks open, and the insects open their wings. After a few hours, the wings dry out and harden, and the dragonflies fly into the sky.

A dragonfly has huge eyes compared to the size of its head. This allows it to spot prey from almost every angle as it flies across the waters of a wetland.

Adult dragonflies have to be great fliers so they can catch enough food to eat. Dragonflies have four wings. They can fly straight up and down, and even hover in midair like a helicopter! As they fly, they catch smaller insect prey such as mosquitoes with their feet.

Flamingos

Flamingos are the most easily recognizable of wetland birds. These bright pink, long-legged birds have huge, curved bills. They live and raise their chicks in shallow lakes.

Long-Legged Birds

Flamingos have long legs to keep their bodies and feathers dry as they walk into deeper water to find food. To feed, a flamingo bends its long, thin neck so that its bill is upside down in the water. Then it sucks in water. As the muddy water passes through the bill, parts inside it work like a filter to trap shrimp and other small animals that the flamingo eats. Sometimes, flamingos stir up the mud at the bottom of a lake with their feet, to bring out more prey!

*Flamingos are not born pink. Their color comes from the **algae** and small shelled animals that they eat.*

HOME SWEET HOME

Flamingos make their nests from a mound of mud, high enough to protect their eggs from flooding. The parents use their bills to pull mud toward their feet to build the nests. They lay one large egg in the nest, and leave a dip at the top so that the egg cannot roll off accidentally.

Shoebills

Shoebills are amazing wetland birds. They stand 5 feet (1.5 m) tall with blue-gray feathers and pale yellow eyes. They are named for their large, oddly shaped bills that look a little like the front of a boot or a clog!

Waiting for Dinner

A shoebill uses its bill to help it eat along the marshy banks alongside rivers. The bill is very thick and heavy, and at the end is a sharp hook. The shoebill stands by the water and waits for small animals such as fish, frogs, turtles, snakes, or even baby crocodiles to swim past. Then it quickly thrusts its head forward to catch the prey in its open bill. The bird uses the sharp edge of the bill to grab the prey and kill it.

The shoebill's bill is 9 inches (23 cm) long and 4 inches (10 cm) wide.

HOME SWEET HOME

Shoebills make their nests among grasses when swamplands are very dry. Unfortunately, this is at the hottest time of the year, so the chicks inside the eggs are at risk of overheating. Shoebill parents use their huge bills to pour water over the nests to keep the eggs cool.

Frogs

Frogs are amphibians. Amphibians are animals that live both in water and on land. Frogs live in wetlands in many places around the world.

Life Under the Water

Frogs start life inside eggs underwater. The tadpoles that hatch out have no legs. They swim by moving their tails. They breathe underwater through special parts called **gills** and feed by grazing on underwater plants. Gradually, they lose their tails, grow **lungs** and legs, and climb out of the water. Adult frogs eat insects, snails, slugs, and other small animals that live near water. They catch prey using their long, sticky tongues and have a lot of tiny teeth to help them grip their food.

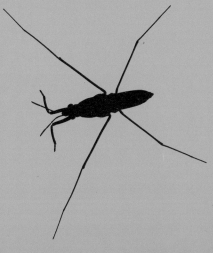

A frog has a flat head with its eyes and nostrils on the top. This allows the frog to see and breathe when most of its body is underwater.

HOME SWEET HOME

On land, frogs use their long back legs to move by jumping. In the water, frogs use their big, **webbed** feet to swim. Webbed feet have skin between the toes. This creates a bigger surface so frogs can push against the water.

Tiger Salamanders

Tiger salamanders are striking animals that are named for their yellow and black tiger-like stripes. These large, solid amphibians grow to about 8 inches (20 cm) long and have strong legs, big heads, wide, round snouts, and small eyes.

Hungry Babies

Female tiger salamanders lay clumps of 100 or more eggs on plants under the water or on the bottom of the wetland. These eggs hatch in about 2 to 6 weeks, depending on how cool or warm the water is. The larvae that hatch eat insect larvae, small, shelled animals, tadpoles, and just about anything they can fit in their mouths! After 10 to 12 weeks, they grow legs, change into adult salamanders, and leave the water for a life on land nearby.

HOME SWEET HOME

Adult tiger salamanders live mainly on land near water. They spend most of their lives underground in deep burrows up to 2 feet (60 cm) below the surface, either in a burrow they have dug themselves or in the burrow of another animal.

Adult tiger salamanders come out of their cool, damp burrows at night to catch worms, insects, frogs, and even other salamanders to eat.

American Alligators

The American alligator lives in warm swamps. This fearsome reptile has about 80 sharp teeth in its long snout, which it uses to catch prey. It is the top predator in the wetland where it lives.

Scaly Bodies

The American alligator's body is covered with a layer of **scales** that are completely waterproof. It has a long, powerful tail that it waves from side to side to help it swim, and it can also stretch out the toes on its webbed feet to help it paddle along. On dry land the alligator uses its four short legs and webbed feet to walk across soft mud without sinking.

If an American alligator loses a tooth when catching tough prey, a new tooth quickly moves in to replace the old one. The alligator can go through thousands of teeth in its lifetime!

An American alligator ambushes birds and other animals that come to wetlands to drink. The alligator's eyes and snout are positioned on the top of its head so it can still breathe and watch for prey while it lies just under the water, out of sight.

Capybaras

Capybaras are about 2 feet (60 cm) tall, making them the biggest rodents in the world. These big, blunt-nosed beasts live and feed on riverbanks, by ponds, in marshes, and in other wetlands.

Strong Swimmers

Capybaras feed on water hyacinths and other water plants, which they bite off with their long, sharp front teeth. They have partly webbed feet that make them strong swimmers, and they make a dash into the water for safety as soon as they spot a predator. They can even take a deep breath and hide below the surface for up to five minutes. Their chubby bodies are designed for water. The fatty layer under the skin acts like a rubber ring and helps them float!

A capybara's teeth continue to grow its whole life. The teeth crop and grind the water plants that the huge rodent grazes on for hours.

HOME SWEET HOME

The capybara's nose, eyes, and ears are all near the top and front of its head. This allows the animal to swim along with only those parts above the water. The capybara can get all the information it needs about its surroundings, smell and see food, and listen out for danger while being mostly hidden.

23

Mudskippers

Mudskippers are wetland fish that can swim in the water, but also spend a lot of time out of it. This allows them to leave the water to find food and also to move between pools of water if one dries up. Mudskippers are named for the way they seem to skip across mud when they move around wetlands.

Swimming and Walking

Just like all fish, a mudskipper's fins help it swim in the water. Out of water, a mudskipper uses its strong tail and fins a little like legs to walk, jump, and climb. It holds its body straight and "jumps" forward on its fins in small skipping movements to move about.

Mudskippers eat a variety of small animals such as insects, small crabs, and worms. Their brown color helps **camouflage** them against the mud while they sit patiently, looking for prey to eat. They use their strong fins to chase victims across the mud.

HOME SWEET HOME

When mudskippers are in the water, they breathe through gills as other fish do. When they climb out of the water, they fill their gills with water so they can take their own oxygen supply onto land.

Manatees

Manatees are sometimes known as sea cows because they are the only mammals that live in water and feed only on plants. These large, gray mammals live in warm coastal wetlands and swim along slowly in shallow water in search of food.

Gentle Giants

The large, gentle manatee has short front flippers and a flat tail for swimming. Sometimes, it uses its flippers to crawl along the bottom of the water. It feeds on beds of sea grass that grow in shallow waters. The manatee has a strong, flexible upper lip that it uses to grasp and rip out whole plants. The manatee is huge so it has to eat a lot of plants to survive. In fact, a manatee can eat one-tenth of its own weight every day!

HOME SWEET HOME

Baby manatees, or calves, are born underwater. At first, the mothers nudge their calves to the surface so that they can take their first breath. Within an hour, manatee calves can swim up and down in the water by themselves.

Manatees can be 13 feet (4 m) long. They never leave the water but they must come to the surface often to breathe.

Wetlands Under Threat

The world's wetlands contain a rich variety of wildlife, but some wetlands are under threat. People drain them to build homes and other buildings or to create farmland. Farmers dig channels to carry water out of wetlands and into their fields. Some wetlands are polluted when chemicals from factories, power plants, or fields wash into them.

Special Places

Wetlands are important places for people. They act like giant sponges, soaking up water and keeping it from flooding land. Wetland plants also filter water and make it clean. Many people are working to protect wetlands. Governments make laws to keep people from taking over wetlands. **Conservation** groups raise money to help protect **endangered** wetland animals such as the Sumatran tiger.

HOME SWEET HOME

Sumatran tigers are found only on the Indonesian island of Sumatra. People are cutting down the trees in swamps where they live to sell as timber or for farmland. Hunters also trap or shoot the tigers for their skin and bones. Today, there are only around 500 Sumatran tigers left living in the wild.

Conservation workers say that their efforts are being successful and that the number of Sumatran tigers is slowly increasing.

Glossary

adaptations Changes to survive in an environment.

algae Plant-like living things that usually grow in damp places.

bark The tough outer layer around the trunk of a tree.

biomes Communities of plants and animals living together in a certain kind of climate.

camouflage A color or pattern that matches the surrounding environment and helps an organism hide.

conservation The act of guarding, protecting, or preserving something.

decay To rot.

endangered When a plant or animal is in danger of dying out.

gills Body parts that fish and some other animals use to breathe underwater.

hatch To break out of an egg.

larvae Animals at the stage when they have just hatched out of eggs.

lungs Body parts that allow land animals to breathe air.

mammals Types of animals that feed their babies with milk from their bodies.

nutrients Chemicals that living things need to live and grow.

oxygen A colorless gas in the air we breathe.

polluted Put something harmful into water, air, or land.

predator An animal that catches and eats other animals.

prey An animal that is caught and eaten by other animals.

reptile An animal group including snakes, lizards, crocodiles, turtles, and tortoises.

rodents Animals with large front teeth for gnawing, such as mice and rats.

roots Plant parts that grow under the ground and take in water.

scales Small, overlapping plates of hard material.

tadpoles Frog larvae.

webbed Having skin between toes or fingers.

Further Reading

Bow, James. *Wetlands Inside Out* (Ecosystems Inside Out).
New York, NY: Crabtree Publishing Company, 2014.

Hinman, Bonnie. *Keystone Species that Live in Ponds, Streams, & Wetlands* (Kid's Guide to Keystone Species in Nature). Hockessin, DE: Mitchell Lane Publishers, Inc., 2015.

Hirsch, Rebecca. *American Alligators: Armored Roaring Reptiles* (Comparing Animal Traits). Minneapolis, MN: Lerner Publishing Group, 2015.

Newland, Sonja. *Wetland Animals* (Saving Wildlife). Mankato, MN: RiverStream Publishing, 2014.

Silverman, Buffy. *Wetlands* (Raintree Perspectives: Habitat Survival). Mankato, MN: Heinemann-Raintree, 2013.

Websites

PowerKids Press has developed an online list of websites related to the subject of this book. This site is updated regularly. Please use this link to access the list: **www.powerkidslinks.com/ahitb/wetlands**

Index